Dark Land, White Light

Early Poems by

David Anthony Sam

Published by Dark Land Publishing

Copyright © 2014 by David Anthony Sam

All rights reserved. Published in the United States of America.

Publication Data

Sam, David Anthony, 1949-

Dark Land, White Light ; poems / by David Anthony Sam – 2nd ed.

ISBN-13: 978-1499623789

ISBN-10: 149962378X

Cover art by Thomas Kuhr

Manufactured in the United States of America

First edition published April 1974

Second edition published May 31, 2014

DEDICATION

To
all who have this
faith
in me.

And to Dennis Stabnau,
who asked to have my first
book dedicated to him
before there was a first word.

D. A. S.
April, 1974

TABLE OF CONTENTS

Poor Tom's a-cold (Or Ten Allusions) _____ 1

Chicago Chrysalis _____ 3

Other Poems _____ 27

    Hawk's Curse _____ 29

    To Hart Crane _____ 30

    7/1/71 _____ 32

    Fugue _____ 33

    Flurries _____ 34

    The Words Flit _____ 35

    Stratford Image _____ 36

    The Moon is a Pale Shadow _____ 37

    Death of a Mountainclimber _____ 38

    Poems for the Center #2 _____ 39

    Poems for the Center #5 _____ 40

    Endnote _____ 41

    Fragment _____ 42

Afterword and Acknowledgements _____ 43

About the Author _____ 44

POOR TOM'S A-COLD
(OR TEN ALLUSIONS)

I write about my own chance,
a poet's prayer,
a poet's dance.
I write to you to see some shape
that lears like me.
I wander words to wander words,
to string my visions with their gods.
I write to you because this song
comes deeper than my plan.

As I mask to have my soul in sound,
I hurl a thousand creatures at some sun.
I throw as many glances
from here within the shadow world
where shadows wander touchlessly.
From their deep skyburning,
a thousand cinders fall into my plate--
my meal for still another quenching thrust.

The visions roll, halfminded,
full of little senses and past rhymes.
Through the background noises
this urging comes
to flounder on a virgin page
to some symphonic clout.

A shadow being, bolted-eyed,
I find the night my time, the sole room,
the vision my only guide through wars
of sounds and flighted patterns.
Burning and crested, a flame-flared wave,
it is my act to hunt for stars
within the grains of scratched sand,
though madness comes into its rage

and rumbles, squeaks, and quivers.

The visions tumble, the music thunders
to an often lean stop. . .
The thing becomes idea becomes a sound
to play on through the naked page
to some blank-faced audience.

In all this formula is strung:
Make a note to hang waved sound
and fill the air with sighted music;
Take a scene to heart and bowl
its atoms out beyond its cost;
Plan the mind into its role,
dress it with the passion, true to blood,
fill it with the motion of the sea,
and curse it with humanity;
Stretch it like a gold sheet,
pound it, melt it, pour it, mold it,
form it to a single breath of wind,
and catch it in a snowbound sterile sheet
with ink characters and violent love.
Then wash it with a month's stare,
cross it with a month's work,
and, if it doesn't melt instead,
freeze it in an envelope.
The event carried, let eyes see.

The visions fold, the sounds lock.
Whether lost within itself,
whether mocks hell of it,
however in disguise I come,
this womb, cradle, bed, grave
is restful when it's done.

CHICAGO CHRYSALIS

"We think our boat is alone,
Rowed through the black night:
Then from the open sea
Comes the plash of paddles"

—from the 8th Century Japanese Poem
"The Embassy to Shinagi"

Tiresias:

From the ledge I watch people,
wandering or surging,
together or sailing alone
by the southern breeze, full-reefed hair.

A she-spirit in a tree tells of the view,
so different, of the sandsorting the waves do,
and of the sorting Rogers Park does:
Old Jews on benches,
baseball in the grass,
lovers and mothers/babies on the walk,
hippies and children in the sand;
kites skirting the sky's tongue,
and waves munching on the beach.

Couples stretch themselves out on the sand,
stretch the sun out on their bare flesh —
dying themselves rich;
dogs bound and mark each tree with urine,
competing.

A fat man in black sunglasses talks to young men.
A girl's hand guides her lovers under her blouse;
another sleeps stoned in the sand,
while friends ponder the delicious bouncing
down along the silky air of grains.

Somehow, seeing it all,
I am inside it all, and yet outside,
alone, lofted like a cloud,
changing shapes and shapeless,
dying each little minute.
Somehow it's all like a thousand times,
and different,
and lost,

and found again under a shattered rock
of memory.

Things go on. I stay.
Things happen, infuse, involve, regress,
sadden, delight, decay;
I stay, unmoving, on a ledge,
watching. There must be a curse.

Quickly,
a coldfingered wind catches the lake's breath
and throws it at the beach,
swiftly slicing,
hitting the kites and trouncing them to the water,
chasing with the dogs,
chasing the sunbathers,
pushing the clouds of individuals away,
leaving me alone with

Night.
The deserted beach cries out;
the waves cry out for me,
thrashing the shore, lashing the pier.
The waves eat sand voraciously,
lacking humans,
but me, stepping bundled into the cold teeth
of the fluorescent flecking bladewaves
and the howling chill breath of the night.
I walk huddled where I wandered warm;
I walk into the waves to retrace
my afternoon footprints, now seaburied dead.

I cast a bleary, weakened shadow on the black water,
Chicago at my back,
my loneliness externalized.
Around me in distorted motions
I see the infra-red shades the others left behind,
wandering the beach despite the cold
and seeking, too, like me, and some finding,

yet, unlike me, and some dying, soon, like me,
all as the churning of the waves makes
the whooshing of the wind a fuel for a machine.

The water calls, but Chicago saves me,
for another night, into its dry womb.
Its life is mine.

narrative

"Get out."

      "Why?"

"Bitch, why did you...?"

      "I love him, too; I love you, too."

"You love nothing. You fill yourself with wine
and smoke and blear at the sight of me.
You run from me to his soft hands.
Why? "

      "I run between you. I love you both. I do."

"Get out. Maybe I'll forgive you…
tomorrow."

Diogenes:

I hear her footsteps clattering the stairs awake,
Making emotion in the dim halls where there's nothing,
Nothing but worn black rubber mats, and worn
Gray (once yellow, once white) wallpaper flowers.
Ungrateful bitch! The hours I spent struggling

To end my silence for short moments of touching;
The endless nights I spent safe, destroyed now.

I see her thru the thin veil of my curtains,
Thru the veil of curtaining midnight mist
Hung in thick curds on the blue-vapor streetlights.
She seems to stumble, uncertain, unclear on her path.
Maybe—maybe she won't run to his lips,
To his flaming madness (She sometimes pretends
To find it in me).

      Now what? What? I guess…
I guess I'll be myself again, unstrung like dirty nylons;
Once more controlled, calm, collecting my dreams
Into their own soft, dirty bag, and shoving them
Out beyond my normal life. At night I can dream,
Realizing that's for night, not for daylight and reality.

I can think myself awake, select a time,
An wake within ten minutes.
I can end this silly daydream gone "heart"-wild!
I can sleep now. Slowly wandering the same dream alleys,
Softly laying my hands thru the things I fear.
But that is all there is to it. That's it.
Dreams don't wake up when you do.

Stupid woman! I could have learned to love… No more!
He is for her—they're alike—I know my place.
It's doing my work. It's seeking hard truth.
It's finding and looking for facts,
Cold, hard, indisputable—unlovable—easily workable
Facts—facts—factum, facti—faccttsss.
I know my—dream, that's all, a dream…I'm feeling…
Stranger. Why have you forsaken me? Pond of blood.
Whose blood? Gouge-eyed monster, coming, coming.
Madness. Speaking—no, dreaming, sleeping, I am….

narrative

The eyes tell gossamer things...
 no words.
She grasps at bolts of
cotton with hands that
touched the edge of ... silence,

    holding out her linen soul

    to ripple by breezes or
        die by flames,
burning like a blowing flag.

As soon as her fate falls
        from the dry clutch of crying
          hands,
        her hands,
he holds the sheath of her hair,
    a robe for fingers,
        a cool red robe to veil hands,
        his hands.

    And thru that link flow
new veins,
new vessels,
new appearances and vials of
feeling,

    while their breathing heaves out
      minute whirls,
        tick by tick, hearts bloat-
          pumping,
    pounding the ground with their
      own sounds.

    Behind one lining,
    lies the flesh, thick,

      toward off winds,
      thin to a lip sucking.

     Behind one flesh,
       they lie enfolded,
wrapped within a column cloud,
red-pinned against the sunset sky,
extension of their hot-blood.

     Exhausted,
       full of each other,
they fall back, grass-trapped,
murmuring against the god
who mounts the wriggling asphalt air,
extension of their hot breath.

Who knows?
However they fly, they fall to life.
No matter how they piece their dream,
the dreams, when stretched, pierce
  them.

            Matin, vesper, evening prayer,
            weave new lights of night,
            strange shapes,
            touch-clinging —
They nominate the flower for a
  mountainship,
and eyes form pyramids of telling.

The eyes tell gossamer things, new
  words,

      and eyes will tell much morning,
      as dew slips, trill-singing, down
soft brows,
         and drowns them.

Dionysus:

I spread my seed in wild, wide
  circles
         that never meet each other,
         concentric,
         elastic, chaotic runnings.
    I crush you, collapse thru you;
    You'll understand.
    You'll see the center, get rid of
        that cemetery thing, "willpower."
    Surrender, dip under the wave.
        Swallow infinity in a minute,
        live it for a night, long,
         silky,
        strange and sensual, full of
        me and you.
Now I come.
Now I leave, away, awake.
I only stay as long as the colors
  melt,
sounds follow like tree-fingers,
the air drifts in smells that drive
  my head
      round and round like swirling
        smoke
           above a fire, hot and dizzy.
    I crush the night
    and swallow myself like a snake,
    spinning, whirring, round, thru
      you.
Then, stop, out, gone.
Packing my life on my back,
hitching thru the dust of an
  expressway,
      feeling the wind of movement
      slip thru and
             pet my flesh,

                        like your hand (now a dead dream,
                        and dream are dead things when
                        done.
            This one's done).
I have to go.
            I don't last long in any place,
                        but I give myself entirely
for the hour, for the night.
You understand. You see me,
            then I go away.
Remember the madness,
            but not for long.
                        Make yourself a
new one.
Feel deeply, kiss everything that
  kisses back,
rush at life, tear its throat,
                        suck the blood from the white
                            flesh,
                        claw at the eyes until they see,
                        hurl yourself into the pain
                        and die.
            Pleasure is life.
            You understand, now: give pleasure.
                        Take it.
Then dissipate your frenzy, but make
                        the dissipation last.
You're dead when you're alive
                                    and not high.

Tiresias:

Ends before beginnings.

I throw myself in my mind to her,
seeing the end coming,
being blinded by it (cold hands),
being bloodied by it — so I
  still and stop,
right at the edge of something,
but something that dies.

So I end it there, safe.
What if I stopped my life, safe,
ended before beginning?

I dream, and watch my dreams perform:
I see her and less familiar beings.
Someone says to us: "Here, spend the
  night,
use this room, use the world."
He, whoever, leaves by a back
  window, smiling,
beatific, kind.
She, Miss Amalgamation, smiles too:
"What a silly idea!" she says;
"What a silly idea." She leaves, said.

Just another dream? yes; not reality.
I have a chance to change that dream.
Still, thinking about it ends it too;
before the dream began,
          the end was planned,
by me.

My head's emptied.
Everyone can see it.
I'm neither cold, nor hot, but

scared.
Too much thought. I can't act.

By myself, withdrawn, alone,
I'm not frightened, nor lonely.
I think and sculpt abstract people
  in clay,
I see things most people ignore,
giant things,
magnificent, beneficent truths of
  things.
Waves enfold my eyes like eyelids.
As an individual one I contact
  this world,
and win.

Why this sudden emptiness at the
  sight,
one woman sitting at a table, sad,
full of faces I never used?
Why a sudden pit opened in my life?

I see a need to join myself.
I see a need to destroy myself.
It's as though, here, now,
with a sight too deep for dreams,
I see my soul formed.
And I see my soul will be female,
                    and when
I meet a female with a male soul,
extinction; antimatter and matter;
plus and minus; water and heat.

But without older (only dead)
  beginnings,
with only ends I built myself and
  fear again,
how can I reach for that?
Or is that, too, a dream, half-felt,

halfwrong?
God! I'm crazy. Why die? What for?
And two ways yet!

The presumption stands;
old, unburied wish,
watered myth-vision;
still I think of it as though a
  substantial fact,
a Fact to be.

Crazy, insane. Sitting at a dinner table,
chewing on a hotdog, thinking —
all destroyed.
              The slick greasy air
  still smells:
the fat truckdriver still leans on
  the stool.
But my dreaming keeps on.
I'm drunk by it.
What am I doing?

She's leaving. How can I pay the way?
I'm only five minutes old.
Without her I don't have a past.
I'm useless.

Alcestis:

How many men are there?
And yet they're all alike —
painful, giving pain
as part of their brave announcements
  of self.

I'm not too smart about life;
still searching for something: what?
Seemingly a man.

A strong, large hand,
a father-figure, a sheltering god?
A wild and passionate hunter?
A force to throw me to completion?
A gentle being, compassionate,
  weak to my strong,
strong to my weak, and neither proud
nor empty?

How many men they are?
I want one, I need one, or some,
And hate them all.
                        Hate is the other
  side
of the same male face of love.
                    Their fast and easy,
their pounding, biting love.
Their words that die with a bed's gasp.
I sometimes think they use
and feel no feeling deeper than the
  groin.
Fat hand, hard face, empty eyes.
The bitterness doesn't last
long enough, though…

Then a someone appears, momently;
he seems too huge to have veins.
He seems alive to knowledge I can't touch;
seems to touch a whole existence.
And, somehow, he wants me, sees in me
something that is more than sweat at night.
And, once again I'm disappointed.
Sure, I put a statue between us,
a figurehead, a golden calf;
yes, I dream of scenes that fail
because of too much thinking.

He fails. Because I dreamed too much?
No; because he flattens himself

before the rolling advertisements
of empty material caricatures of things,
or before the darkness of his own ego.

I often think they use me,
like a sweetsmelling bedsheet,
use until I yellow, and then throw out.
And the need I have is nothing here.

            Then I clasp the emptiness,
I see the gulf of my death,
I see the half of me that isn't
over the grinning black chasm edge
of my gently creaking bed.

Whoever he was, he's gone, still beside me,
or walking into another bedroom,
he's not in me, part of Us;
he's a separate shell with a wry face
and a willing wallet (if needed).

And I keep on dreaming, too deep;
I see my soul is unformed,
unshaped but slowly growing as I die.
And I see my soul must be a male.
And I know I have to fall together,
as he must fall together, thinking,
  feeling, dreaming.

  Yes, dreaming, I am, walking home,
lonely, empty-lonely, standing,
   waiting,
watching neon mouths flash teeth,
seeing cars bleed taillights one way,
pierce the night with hot tongues of
  white light the other.

The edge of the curb, a blade,
like the edge of my bed,

the edge of my pain, my stupid
  wishing.
Over it is the gulf — if I fall,
        just right, my head will smash
              against the soft caress of a
              speeding car,
                  steel comfort...

                      How many men there are?
When they see my blood on the cement,
they might be terrified, and cry.
If they would, there'd be no poem
  there.

Tiresias:

Am I a lemming or a phoenix?
Somehow I feel her pain, this woman
washed up on the shore like a raft,
into my worn out hands, crying.
How do I fall so quickly into her life,
crying her tears? Do I have the right?
Yes, if I do, why don't,
why can't I think her words and understand?
I understand more.
What symbiosis or twice-removed self-pity
makes me absorb her and touch her eyes,
though I've been blinded?
My own deceit and empty dreaming
stand like old stories here,
brownyellow crumblings, useless.
Her lungs nearly refused to breathe,
so heavy with the shell of her life.
What is the woman for? What can I do?
She lives — alright — then what am I,
an empty canister to pour her pain in?
And what is she to me?

narrative

Caught in an Orphean dream,
eyes fallow in the faltering of eyes,
pinpoints out of reach,
her face tightened by fake muscles,
her vision of a dead world of shallow colors
suddenly aroused to fever,
she clutches at her lips,
feels the motion of her words,
hears only no one's silence,
dies into the vision, sightless.

Slowly, her face catches the corner
  of a bureau,
her blood trickles slightly,
she echoes memories on the soft
  carpet.

All actions are perverse.
Hers are mixed with the sublime,
but still bent.

A bottle neck becomes a throat;

a man who is a woman follows her
with silent reaching steps.

He stops before her fallen clothes
and burns them.
Flames arouse a dark light in his
  eyes,
pools of blood!

He touches for her hair,
but she can only scream and run
  from that,
back to her melted world.

She runs from the Cheshire cat,
she runs from the outstretched.
Soft and gentle, loving both,
   she runs between
the world and the dream,
   crashing between,
seldom living,
running in between.

Hating nothing but the dull ache
   of loneliness,
fearing only her need and its
   success,
she seeks to feel by being felt,
she tries to use herself —
   she must run.

The woman is a girl and dead —
she is a kind of bed for hot men;
only, broken on the beach by passions,
half crumbling sandstone,
half burning tissue,
only, like a wave collapsing on
   herself, alive,
and running between.

She stops. She must stop.
The soft touch startles her, seeking
   deeper
than her musk skin, but thru it —

The roles spin between them.

He touches her again,
without claws, without cold
   tentacles;
he is between the running now.
Returned from a hell-pillared cave,
seeing two different ways with both

  eyes,
having roots deep in other nerves,
he sails the breathe of everyone he
  meets,
he sees in puddles reflections of the sun,
now,
where before he saw mud;
and he tells.

The woman is awakened, slowly;
the damp cloth helps.
Cold water clutters her eyes.
Her head stuffs itself with pain.
Still the hands don't run away.
He stays between,

between her and the door which
  hides the alley
(from whom?). For whom?
She softens back to sleep.
Still the hands can't leave.
A man who is a man must join with her.
A man who is a man is a woman.

Them:

There's so much hell in this.
Knowing that I love you.
Knowing that I don't, and can't
and can, and do, and am, and was;
Sweaty touch spring much,
garbled eyes glow fine, clear,
bright as golden grass, shining,
  shivering,
in-living so much more than dying
normally—
              Normally is Dying.

Dying into you, living is dying.
Is living.
Entire, alone; alone, inside, and
out.
Nodding at the wisdom tree,
layer on unplanned layer leaf,
leaves a thousand miles deep to
the sky.
Branches over branches inside branches.
Shouting out leaves, feeling the air,
touching your face, feeling the wetness,
the warmth, alone, us alone, we alone,
Alone, but empty of myself.
I am not lonely.

You touch too many ways,
too deeply, too far, too well.
The inside of my curtain bleeds.
It is your bleeding.
Where are you? Which am I?

Explosion.
Separation.
Dreamimage on a mind mirror
playing the scene.
Where are you?
Inside, but only part.
One fingertip touches me — Where
are you?
The whole should touch at once,

It does.
I am an atom to a bouncing atom,
molecules of madness, life-giving
  living
in the breast of death.
Death breathes life through your lips.
It gives the life to life,
makes it alive to living the life

of death.

You are the one that is outside,
fighting to get in.
I am the outside in me trying
to get out and into myself who
  is you.

Once it was easy, dead, done, masked
in done death.
Now I love, feel the whole thing,
find rivers of sense to everything,
confused and floundering.

I am the one and nothing both,
You are me, one and nothing both,
hate and love, both, beauty and
  despair, both,
death and life, both, all and all
  there is.
We do this to little sane children
and drive them mad in us.
We are we, no wonder what.

Tiresias:

We brushed the back of the mountain only,
not really high enough to break the sky
and turn it into storm.
And still it rains of us.

Down, down, down, the rushing rain,
beads of life.
All is gone: exhaustion, separation,
all trail sheetwash into rivulets of mud.
From the large, gray, hidden clouds
veins of lightning shoot,
echoing our dying bloodstreams,

brief imitations of a hidden sun
along the edges of rolling, grumbling clouds.
The light glows on the wet hairstrips
that coat your back like seaweed;
The storm is the motion of our living breath,
drawn from the massed choir clouds
as it was pulled into our aching lungs.
Cackling, the witch storm plays our love,
toying passion, longer, huger.

In the darkness between flashes I
am alone again.
But somehow, seeing it all,
I am inside it all, living it all
feeling each slap of thunder like pain,
aching each rain dropped like death,
joying in the joy lightning,
laughing with the storm's sounds.

Above, lofted like a cloud,
changing shapes and shapeless,
living each little minute.
Somehow it's all like a thousand lives,
and different,
and lost,
and found again, lived again
under the memory.
The curse died even as we did.
It can never live again; we can.

Night.
You cried out to me, I to you.
We met, lived each other, and more.
That can never die; it lives like a wave
growing, surging, collapsing, then withdrawing,
followed by another, alike, individual,
sea memories forever,
sea lives forever.
The water calls me to life.

I follow you there.

I have to sing higher than my voice.
The force of a million lives, a whole,
is behind everything felt.
You saved me to save you
to find everything. So easily found.

It was a dream, unfinished, not fully
touched,
lost sometimes in images of grizzled
obsessions,
somehow dreamt with real touches.
Dreams never die while the dancer dances,
the poet sings, and the world whirls
in tangles of lives.
Despite broken eyes, despite old hands,
flesh pale from empty clutchings,
despite dead lives, we were.
Life lives when we do.
Here in words, what I am, you are,
we all are, they are, alive.

Within the eldest soul you are
that grows within the two that we,
grows the tree; within the fibrous reachings
that do not join as much as find
old joinings, there we are,
the center that doesn't have to be,
and is nothing but is.
We take a part and separate.
The dream (real or reality) shows
us to the center.
There we have to go, to the soul,
through the song of life.

The soul, we are, is God,
we are, the soul.
And all is poetry.

Your lives are mine.
And all are poetry.
We are better children by the collision.
Is the dream dead so soon?
No — we are just dead to it.

Life will come again.

OTHER POEMS

Hawk's Curse

Fly higher, bird, seek topclouds,
feel vertigaining air.
Fly higher, fill with
brief, long-aching sights.
When you're blasted from the sky
by a bloodthurst of shot
from a mindless demongun,
drink in sunfire and die there,
high, with Icarian wings melting,
and with the rent chest
bleeding life into the hawk's curse.

To Hart Crane

"If we're drunk enough, someone dances a jarabe."
– Hart Crane

But how long can you dance, tired,
exhausted by your weaves of steps,
each torn from aching muscles
like words ripped from an angry throat?

(The astrologer said,
"Salt water.")

The sun dies in the Caribbean.
The water bristles at the bow,
steam shooting off the ship sides;
Oblivion waits below, the sea,
the aching arms of the begging sea.
Dull gray-black smoke trickles from
some impotent and dirty stacks.

(Put a record on the Victrola and sing,
ears buzzing from the long hung sound.
I will, but how long can you dance…)

The bridge, wasted without anyone crossing,
wasted unless my bridge is walked
when I'm dead. Death…
the wave hits the ship side.

I say YES, yes to complete life,
yes to complete death, but nowhere between,
no lame lingering on the bridge of the ship
like on the edge of the suspension span
between one troubling cliff
and another, dark and skytoothed —

The water seems warm enough,

pleasant really in the blind lungs breathing
only the fingers of death, soft,
gentle, coming with my lover's eyes.
(I will, I say YES!)

And fall, Porphyro in aching,
to the voyage of the last caress, silence.

7/1/71

People think you own the trees,
or these pieces of earth,
even graves to deed the ground —
I don't own any of these; I merely touch them.

So I could be with you, If I were
the better child I should be,
not a grabbing child, but a touching child.

Even this poem is no more mine
than the soft pelt puff you would feel
if I stroked your arm, or breast.
This is a touch, and a touch cannot be owned.
It can only be opened.

You are the thing to be touched,
and I can't own you.
Open yourself to me.

Our sweet electric moisture,
and the gentle wind of breathings,
and the caress of your soul against mine
are infinitely mortal and eternally dying touches.
Who is the god?

Together let's be one touch
caressing the lithe back of the earth's grass,
separating so the touch can be again.

Fugue

The single field sprouts blankfaced archers,
lined in arithmetic line, signful,
brave in bowheld intimation
of secrets held inside the belly earth.
They loose white lucent pure light arrows
against invisible immortals,
a phallus flock,
a whoosh of signing at the sun
to die embedded in Valhalla corpses.
Blood billows
for the greentongued earth to lap alive.

Flurries

She came in sideways glances,
Glimmerings of bright words
And songs of free motions in the snow.
She crushed the fortress walls,
Then threw her gaze elsewhere, quickly,
Without the silence of cold words.
Like Adam's God she touched my hand
And threw me free to the death's end.
I, left with soothed scalp bruises,
Am stretched too thin, too empty;
Her voiding wake has too much to fill.
She leaves a fluorescent trail to watch,
Like a slow sea ship, just passed,
While a dingy lingers on a wave,
Post-tossed and troughed within.

The Words Flit

The words flit with my lips.
They sound slowly.

Some eyes turn,
some sleep, some bellow.
It's like walking into a stadium,
stripping off any clothes, standing nude,
then stripping off the outer flesh
and standing soul-bare;
and saying, "This is what I am.
This is all, this is all,"
and then crying softly on my needs.

Yet my soul has flown out
to be a little bit of other lonely souls,
listening.
Then I cry softly,
on my strengths, aloud,
crying words for other people's tears,
and mine, yes, and mine,
saying, "This is all, this is all,
all of us, all we are."

Then the words are yours as much as mine.

Stratford Image

While the sun sets behind a cloud,
a white swan, water god, comes,
peers his sharp-eyed silent song at me,
dances his slowmotion chant,
flippers off, west, and the sun
rises from behind a golden crescent cloud
and crowns his head in yellow.

The Moon is a Pale Shadow

The moon is a pale shadow,
leaves shiver in the wake.

Crack, sigh, crash, one dies,
one of everything dies in order...

Even the wind sighs.

Hear his feet, crackling the earth,
tumbling in the motions of a crumbling leaf.

Words are quiet sun songs,
tumbling in the motions of his rising steps.

At the top of the hill the moon is
still waiting above once taller trees.
He sees the moon set twice.

His pale shadow staggers alone.

Leaves wonder in his wake.

A sound is missing.

Death of a Mountainclimber

I feel the oldness finalize within me,
white as glass chip ice,
and I follow the bone track home.
I am going now.

High, a last climb, a last series
of handgrasps, a last ringing of steel,
a last living above the clouds;
I am going now.

The steeple cliffs sing silently,
reaching (as I've always done) higher,
pointing stone Gothic intonations to lead my eyes.
Before, when I reached the top,
the world continued below,
but I had grappled beyond it.
In the past, when I have found my soul,
it was alone on a peak.

Now I am going,
a mourner and a celebrant both.
I pass the last living — the tree line.

The brown rock and the blueburning glacial snow
split the world off from the peaks.
I pass the world to the peak.
Here, alone, I'll find my soul,
the soul that was never soft-touched
but often knew the love of ice and cold-clawed rock.

Here, alone, I'll leave my flesh
to tumble with the glacier
and melt its unity below.

Poems for the Center #2

Deep.
Pinholes cut in a shoebox — stars.
Ball on the end of string — world.
Deep. Deep. Deeping.

He filled his mouth with the ether,
felt the blackness flood his blood
with the spacemad surges of birth.
A head comes, his, silent, bluecheeked,
stillborn world coming,
the steelblue gates split,
spit out a question of a life,
spinning, screaming coagulation,
whirring out vapor absence.
The gates close,

Deep,
the soul is lost in the chaos.
Deeper,
the body drags the empty flesh shroud.
Deeper,
the poles of light gleam,
announcing the center,
the hole in the blacksea game,
the finish of the birthgot race,
bellowing hot silence
Deeper
than the question that has come.

The blueborn child bleeds,
his heart becomes,
his scream echoes the air gush,
and the end is begun
in the deepest center of the absence.

Poems for the Center #5

All the watchings melt,
smooth into some silence,
calm, distort.
The candle plays streaks and spots
off the inside of my eyes,
swallows itself to my sleep.

All the sounds soothe
into one silence.
All the silences remember music.
A piano sings.
The dusk of a room's night
smells of candle smoke;
drips of energies of memories congeal.

All the motions still
into the wave of my life
touching from shore to shore,
smooth water rolling wave to wave,
forever whispering my love.
Infinity in the blackness under my feet,
the Center in a wick halo,
and the music.

Endnote

Fire

takes the world to ashes.
Red crackling lips
melted Beowulf into destruction.

Fire

took Emily's hands
to the end of life-emotions,
fire to ashes,
ashes to ashes,
ashes to fire.

Visions lurk coaleyed
behind the torch of every pen
to every firehungry page.
This bluelined wordflesh
waits for the smoke to raise it
into infinite winds,
like an island's explosion of eternal sunset.

Fire

hates the word
and fears it on to life.

Fire

veins the mountain
with the lava of ages
searching for the tree.

Fragment

From the joinings of the past
comes the call, coming wordlessly,
The urge to wander aimlessly
the countryside and sing,
A new Deor, only fresh, not cut off,
singing to the tribes that come together.
My voice is weak, hesitant;
Some little fear holds my feet.
If I don't begin the walk, I'll die again.
If I do, what then?
How long can your machines and cars,
How long can your mad air,
your war planes hovering like insane bees,
your cave cities; how long can your iced eyes
Stand my half-poetic cries,
forgive my small madness?
From the joinings of the past, I must.
From the fear I almost cannot.
But I do walk here to the ridge of your eyes.
That is what this is.
That is what I am:
A reaching thru a page to your eyes.

Afterword and Acknowledgements

This collection was originally self-published as a chapbook in April 1974. It was done the old-fashioned way: I typed it myself on folded sheets of paper, penciled with page numbers so I would get it right. The cover was a wood carving by Tom Kuhr, then inked and pressed to paper. The entirety was printed on a photo-offset machine by Richard Dine (since deceased), another friend who happened to own a print shop at the time. Poet William R. Allen and I worked together on our two volumes, and folded the collated paper to bind using a saddle stapler I had purchased and still own somewhere in the basement.

The poems were written between 1970 and 1973 when I was in my early twenties They are juvenilia, for certain, but some of them hold up fairly well after all these years. Most are here printed exactly as they were in 1974. I have made minor edits to a few to correct only the most clumsy parts.

The author circa 1972

About the Author

Born in Pennsylvania, David Anthony Sam is the grandchild of immigrants. He has lived in Michigan, Florida and now resides in Virginia with his wife and life partner, Linda. They have two children and three grandchildren. Sam has written poetry for over 40 years and has been published in various journals and has one new collection of poems , Memories in Clay, Dreams of Wolves. He serves as president of Germanna Community College and writes poetry that seeks to understand the unity of all being.

The author 2014